In appreciation
Saw Dough Air Show 2001
Jack & Myrna Kingrati

YUKON
by Northern Light

YUKON
by Northern Light

R. WAYNE TOWRISS

Published by
Studio North Ltd.
Whitehorse, Yukon

Fifth edition 1999
Copyright © 1983 — **R. W.** Towriss

ISBN 0-88925-453-2

Printed in Canada by
D. W. Friesen and Sons Ltd.
Altona, Manitoba

A Yukoner is . . .

Does it take a residency of five years, ten years, or even 25 years? Is it a membership in YOOP, the Yukon Order of Pioneers? Do you have to be born on Yukon soil?

Those who call themselves "Yukoners" are often quite individualistic. They are proud of their accomplishments. They are proud of their way of life and they are proud of little differences; often justifiably so. Some may also be just a little touchy about who uses the title.

To me, "being a Yukoner" is a thing of the heart. One does not have to wrestle a grizzly bear or even "see the Yukon ice go out". It requires only a love of the land and an appreciation of her moods and beauties.

This book is dedicated to all Yukoners — wherever they may live.

R. Wayne Towriss

Fireweed

Introduction

"Outsiders" and "cheechakos" usually have a preconceived picture of Yukon. In many cases it is a sharp, definite image; a flat, cold image. In most cases it is wrong.

Contrary to common belief, the territory is not covered with ice and snow year round. It is not grey and bleak. Yukon is a colourful land. Its winters, pastel pink and blue; its summers, a thousand shades of green; and autumn, a palette of primaries.

Focus on the northwest corner of Canada — right up against Alaska, just north of British Columbia. Yukon is the most westerly part of Canada. The majority of it lies west of Vancouver Island. The Yukon picture, still, is a northern picture. In the Beaufort Sea white Beluga Whales patrol its north coast. It is, however, not the typical northern image. Crop out the igloos, the eskimos and almost all of the Polar Bears. They are part of the Alaska picture, or maybe that of the Northwest Territories.

Look again. Much of the Yukon is tundra, it is true, but it is not flat. Enlarge the mountains. No! Even Larger! Along the western boundary, the St. Elias Mountains contain some of the highest peaks on the North American continent. Its glaciers form non-polar icefields that are second to none.

Criss-cross your image with rivers; miles of rivers, filled with salmon and Arctic Grayling. Rivers with names like Teslin, Takhini, Tatshenshini; names like Dezadeash, Nordenskiold, and Nisutlin. Some with native Indian names, some with names of the first white explorers. Include the Yukon River, fourth longest on the continent. As you can now begin to see, this is no small picture. And there is more — much more. Along these waterways lay gold pans and paddlewheelers; remnants of an era when the world literally revolved around this area. The gold-bearing gravel of the Klondike drew over 40,000 men and women to Dawson City at the turn of the century. Although today, gold isn't as big a drawing card, each summer it still brings hundreds to muck and scrabble under the midnight sun. It also draws thousands more to watch.

The territory's wide-angled wilderness teems with wildlife. Dall Sheep peer down from the mountain crags. The moose, the wolf and the last of the world's grizzly bears populate the valleys. The tundra of the north, above the Arctic Circle, is the summer home of the Porcupine Caribou herd — 100,000 strong.

Yukon's skies are filled with eagles, Peregrine Falcons, and Trumpeter Swans. Birds of every size, shape and color, rush each spring to get the best nesting sites in the north. Beneath the shimmer of winter's northern lights clucks the snow-white ptarmigan. As temperatures plummet, his coal-black cousin, the raven, heads for the garbage cans of the nearest settlement.

Settlements? Yes, there are people in this picture. Not many by some standards (maybe 25,000) about one-third of native ancestry and two-thirds, white. Some live in log cabins in the bush, but over half have bungalows or modern split-level homes in the capital city of Whitehorse. The rest spread out in smaller communities throughout the territory.

The people are miners and millwrights; trappers and truckers. They are cashiers and can-can girls.

Some are even photographers. In his own way, each as colourful as September buckbrush.

Now, touch-up your picture with a few clichés; a few howling huskies, a few more beards and maybe another gold nugget or two. Bonanza! There you have it! You have developed a panorama of the Yukon that is 300,000 kilometres square; a panorama that is constantly changing.

Sunlight filters through the mountain tops, altering the tint of sky and horizon by the second. Glassy lakes are wind-whipped into a roaring froth in minutes. By the day, roads, power lines and cities change the face of the land. New Yukoners are born. Others come and go with the seasons. All are part of the mosaic.

The Yukon picture takes many forms. Sometimes from a poet's pen, sometimes from the brush of an artist, and sometimes, even from the epistle of a bureaucrat. This one is captured through a piece of Japanese optical glass. It is yours to enjoy.

Watson Lake Signposts

The Alaska Highway near Haines Junction

Siberian Phlox

Lapie Lake/South
Canol Road

Evening on Teslin Lake

Trumpeter Swans on Marsh Lake

*Kluane Game
Sanctuary*

13

*First buds on
Sheep Mountain*

*Dall rams in
Kluane Park*

Arctic Willow

Jackson Lake
near Whitehorse

17

*Whistler Swans
on Schwatka
Lake*

*Purple Mountain
Saxifrage*

*Kluane National
Park*

Dall ram

Grizzly
Bear/Ursus
Horribilis

*Windswept
Kathleen
Lake/Kluane Park*

Yellow Pond Lily

26

Summer
waders

Afloat on the
Wheaton

Paddlewheeler Tutshi

Matthew Watson General Store/Carcross

Carcross Desert

Remains of Venus Mill

Windy Arm/Tagish Lake

The marge of
Lake Lebarge

Midnight on
Kluane Lake

*Deserted cabin
near Carmacks*

*Macmillan
River/North
Canol*

Early morning crystals

Frosty moose pasture

Frost's Handiwork

*Freeze-up on
Kusawa Lake*

*Sundog over
Ogilvie
River/Dempster
Highway*

A Rose hip snack

Winter's icy grip

"It's The Best"

Yukon was the best there was. It was the turn of the century. Times were changing and Dawson City was the place to be.

Since the big discovery of 1896, men and women from every corner of the globe had been trying to get to this bit of northern muskeg. They clawed their way over mountain passes. They slogged their way through hundreds of miles of mud and mosquitoes. They fought river ice, their whip-sawn boats often sinking under them. Some 40,000 made it. Newspapers around the world were full of their exploits; their adventures covering the front pages. Riches were in the Klondike for the taking. Most didn't know just where the Klondike was, but they did know that they should be there.

As soon as George Carmacks, Tagish Charlie and Skookum Jim let out the news, men started working to make Dawson City the biggest thing in the northwest. They succeeded beyond their wildest dreams. They packed organs and eggs over the Chilkoot on their backs. They trained tons of mining supplies and food produce on the newly constructed White Pass and Yukon Route railway, then steamed it down the river

Daybreak on the Dempster.

by paddlewheeler. Caviar and wine, roulette wheels, dance hall girls and the finest in lace came around Alaska and up the river from the north. By 1900, the shops were filled with Paris fashions; libraries bulged with the latest books. The saloons had the best champagne available; the Palace Grand Theatre, the best in entertainment. Dawson was booming. Men had gold, and second best just wasn't good enough.

Most of those in the big rush of '98 were too late. They had left families and friends, spent every cent they had, and suffered untold hardships; only to find that all the good gold-bearing land was staked before they arrived. It didn't matter. Many didn't even leave Dawson for the goldfields on the creeks. They had made it! They were the hub of the world and they knew it. The gold wasn't important anymore.

Today, many of the frills are gone and the territory's population has dropped by half, but the goldrush aura and Yukon's natural splendor remain. People still come from around the world. Each year, thousands head for the Yukon and adventure. Thousands more live in the territory and couldn't be happier. To most of them, "Yukon is still the best there is."

Remnants of the Gold Rush/Dawson City

53

Today's Dawson

Captain Dick

"O.D." Brown

———

Diamond Tooth
Gertie's

#4 Dredge on
Bonanza

Old Klondike
Cabin

Silver City

Chiming Bells

Wild Crocus

———

Nootka Lupine

Barrenground Caribou

Arctic Cotton at rainbow's end

Dragon Lake
Area/North Canol

Colours on the
Rose River

S.S. Klondike/
Whitehorse

City Centre

S.S. Klondike/
Whitehorse

40° below on the
Yukon River

Mushing Home

After the Race

Listen . . .

You can hear a Yukon spring arrive. It arrives with the tinkle of candle ice on Kluane Lake, the model-T-like honk of a Trumpeter Swan at Tagish and the shrill whistle of a Hoary Marmot in the high mountains.

It's late, at least by most Canadian standards. The ducks, geese and swans (both Trumpeter and Whistler Swans) begin to arrive in the head-waters of the Yukon River system in early April. By mid-month the lone goose call has become a din as thousands of waterfowl stage on the ice-free portions of Marsh and Tagish Lakes, awaiting breakup further north.

It's a slow process. The ice is not totally off the larger lakes until mid June, but by then most of the birds are well on their way to Arctic nesting grounds, using each open puddle to feed and then push north.

In the mountains the grizzlies are out early, tossing boulders in search of a fat, tasty ground squirrel. By the end of May, spindly, little Dall lambs scramble after mother. On Sheep Mountain, at the end of Kluane Lake, the rams move from the low spring grass and crocuses, up and over the front peaks and on to summer pastures, deeper in the range.

On the lake itself, ice a metre thick begins to rot and break down into long candle-like crystals that tinkle like wind chimes.

Winter's snow has been off the lower elevations for weeks. Days are long, sunny and warm, yet it is the end of May before the yellow-green buds burst on the cottonwoods. In the high country, snow crowns the peaks all summer long. Deep inside the St. Elias Range it packs, year after year, creating glaciers and ice fields that bulldoze the landscape into new vistas.

By mid-summer, eagles scream overhead, while the sheep, goats and caribou nibble flowers in the mountain meadows. Cow moose lead their wobbly offspring into ponds to avoid the bite of black fly and mosquito. Grayling "blip" as they take the insects off the water's surface.

July brings highways lined with the pink of Yukon's floral emblem. Fireweed fields fill the ditches as if planted by some giant hand. In the north, along the

Heading South

Dempster Highway and around Dawson City, hills are cloaked in white-tuffed cotton grass. Noon temperatures reach 30°C.

By August the bull moose sport new, moss-covered racks. On the mountains the blueberries are ripe and the bearberry is scarlet. Frost, or maybe even a skiff of snow, may greet the early rising hiker.

By the first week of September, summer is over, and the autumn colors are something to behold. Aspens in the Klondike turn the hills to gold. One of the best areas to enjoy fall's foliage is along the Canol Road. There, entire mountains are arrayed in red.

Two more weeks and the leaves are gone. The bull moose are in full rut, stamping and grunting along the roadsides, spoiling for a fight. Canada Goose congregate on Sheldon and a thousand other lakes, strengthening their wings for the long flight south. Caribou wander the ridges in full fall dress — huge sweeping antlers and sparkling white capes. Sandhill Crane string overhead in wave after honking wave.

October's earth is brown and frozen. Snow creeps down the mountain slopes a little further each day. Swans, some of the last migrants to leave, dot Quiet Lake and lesser bodies of water on the South Canol, as well as Finlayson and Frances Lake, further east on the flyway. By month's end the Canol is blocked with snow and the martin that inhabit the area are donning winter furs.

On the Dempster at Halloween you can often hear the clicking hooves of thousands of barrenland caribou, arriving on wintering grounds, after a long trek from the north coast. Temperatures regularly dip to −40°C.

November's winds drive snow into the southern part of the territory as well. There is one last mad dash of activity. Dall rams bash heads for harem supremacy. Rodents try to squirrel away just one more mouthful of food, and trucks head to the bush for that last load of firewood. The strong of heart wax cross-country skis and tune snow machines. Others book for Maui.

The Yukon is again locked in winter's icy grip.

About the Author

Wayne Towriss had his first photograph published over 20 years ago. Since then his work has appeared in print around the world.

His photos have been in National Geographic, Time, Macleans, Canadian Geographic, and Alaska Magazine — to name a few. They have also graced the pages of most of the major newspapers of Canada, as well as many in the U.S. and overseas.

Raised in Saskatchewan, Wayne is a former newspaper reporter and editor. Since arriving in Yukon 12 years ago he has spent his weekends and evenings travelling trails and backroads, enjoying the many pleasures Yukon has to offer, and, at the same time, working to obtain the images for this publication.